MagicMoonPublish

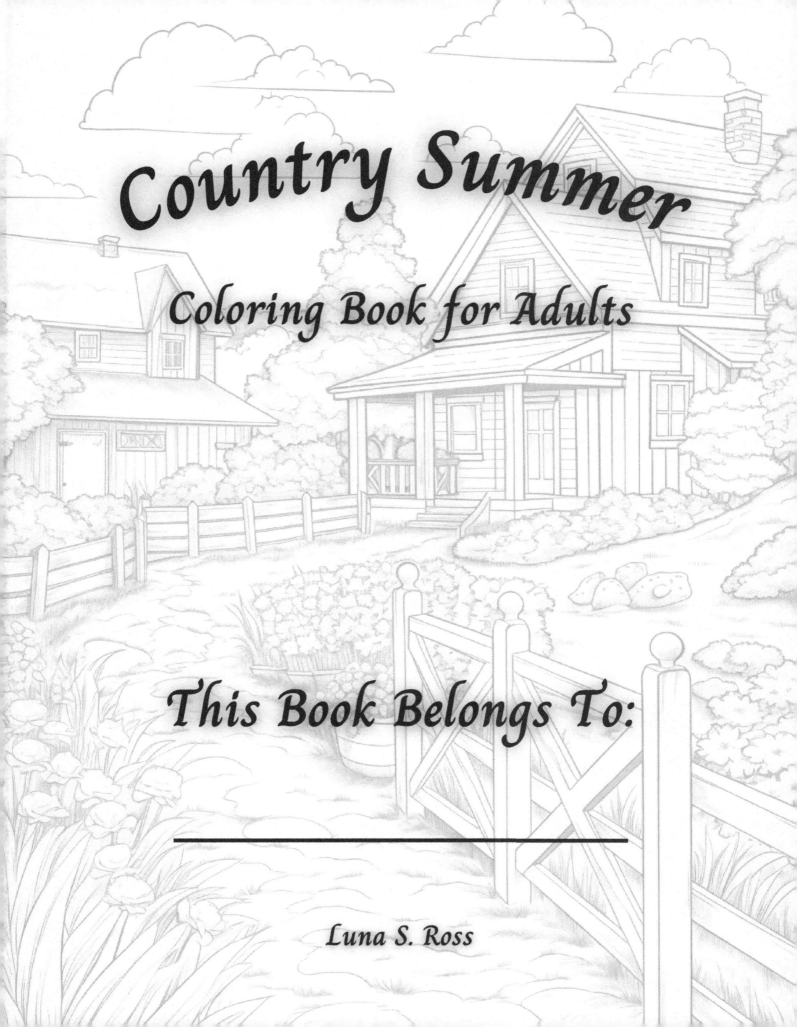

Country Summer

Coloring Book for Adults

This Book Belongs To:

_____

Luna S. Ross

Thank you

We hope you enjoyed our book.

As a small company, your feedback is very important to us. Please let us know how you like our book with a review on Amazon or at:

magicmoonpublish@gmail.com

Made in the USA
Las Vegas, NV
22 December 2023

83454063R00059